CREATIVE COMPANIES

THE STORY OF
DISNEY

VALERIE BODDEN

JAICO PUBLISHING HOUSE

Ahmedabad Bangalore Chennai
Delhi Hyderabad Kolkata Mumbai

Published by Jaico Publishing House
A-2 Jash Chambers, 7-A Sir Phirozshah Mehta Road
Fort, Mumbai - 400 001
jaicopub@jaicobooks.com
www.jaicobooks.com

Published in arrangement with
The Creative Company
123 South Broad Street, Mankato, MN 56001, USA

To be sold only in India, Bangladesh, Bhutan,
Pakistan, Nepal, Sri Lanka and the Maldives.

Design and Production by Zeno Design

Photographs by Alamy (Allstar Picture Library, Content Mine International, Blaine Harrington III, Jon Arnold Images Ltd, Richard Levine, LHB Photo, Alan Myers, M. Timothy O'Keefe, Photos 12, Pictorial Press Ltd, Chris Wong, www.white-windmill.co.uk), Corbis (Paul Almasy, Bettmann, Jonathan Blair, Douglas Kirkland)

THE STORY OF DISNEY
ISBN 978-81-8495-772-3

First Jaico Impression: 2015
Sixth Jaico Impression: 2019

Page design and layout: Special Effects, Mumbai

Printed by
Trinity Academy For Corporate Training Limited, Mumbai

CREATIVE COMPANIES

THE STORY OF DISNEY

When brothers Roy and Walt Disney opened the Disney Brothers Studio in Hollywood in 1923, their goal was modest: to make animated films. They began with a couple thousand dollars (most of it borrowed), a second-hand camera, and little else. What they ended up with was an entertainment empire now known as the Walt Disney Company. Today, that company does business around the world, earning more than $34 billion a year. From its humble beginnings, it has expanded to encompass film studios, theme parks, a cruise line, television and radio networks, record labels, publishing houses, and retail stores. Yet, despite its incredible growth, the Walt Disney Company is perhaps still most famous for the animated character who got it all started: Mickey Mouse.

1
In Search of Success

When 21-year-old Walt Disney decided to move from Kansas City, Missouri, to Hollywood, California, he hadn't yet even dreamed of Mickey Mouse. He had created other cartoon characters for Laugh-O-Gram Films, the Kansas City company he co-owned with a friend, but after the company went bankrupt, Walt found himself discouraged from animation.

Yet, unable to find a job after he arrived in Hollywood, he once again turned to drawing cartoon and soon convinced his older brother Roy, who was recovering from tuberculosis in a Los Angeles hospital, to join him in opening their own studio. The two brothers quickly established the Disney Brothers Studio in a small, windowless office and began work on *Alice's Wonderland*, a series of films that featured a real girl in a cartoon world.

Although the brothers made little money that first year, they were confident, and with his typical optimism, Walt told his father that he would "make the name Disney famous around the world." Although he at first produced much of the company's animation, Walt soon realized that there were other artists more talented than he and turned instead to directing the animators that the studio hired. As Walt focused on the creative side of the company, Roy dealt with the financial aspects of running a business, trying to keep Walt—who rarely worried about money—

on a budget. In 1926, Walt and Roy decided to rename their company Walt Disney Productions (which later became the Walt Disney Company), as they believed it would help business if people thought a single individual had created their films.

Even with the new name, the company at first struggled to sell enough films to pay its few employees. Then, in 1927, the Disneys created Oswald the Lucky Rabbit, who became an instant success. People around the country flooded theaters to watch Oswald's latest antics—from racing airplanes to hunting big game in Africa—and items with Oswald's floppy-eared picture on them filled store shelves. Confident that the company had at last gotten its big break, Walt and his wife, Lilly headed to New York to negotiate a new contract with their distributor, fully expecting to get more money for the little rabbit. Instead, Walt was offered less money and was told that all but one of the company's animators had been hired away. What was worse, the distributor, Universal Pictures—not Walt Disney

Alice's Adventures in Wonderland, a story written in 1865, inspired the first Disney cartoon films

Productions—owned the rights to Oswald.

Disappointed but never one to give up, Walt boarded the train back to California and began to doodle. Soon, a mouse with large, round ears had "popped out of [his] mind and [onto] a drawing pad." Walt asked his wife if she liked the name "Mortimer Mouse." She suggested that he name the character "Mickey Mouse" instead, and, in that instant, one of the most famous cartoon characters of all time was born.

In May 1928, the first Mickey Mouse cartoon, a six-minute film called *Plane Crazy*, was previewed in Hollywood, and a second short, *Gallopin' Gaucho*, soon followed. Although the films were received with some enthusiasm by the Hollywood crowd, no one was

Walt Disney's company seemed destined for greatness once he created his signature character, Mickey Mouse willing to distribute them. The Disneys knew they had to do something special to get Mickey Mouse noticed. Only a few months before, the first-ever motion picture with sound had been introduced, and now Walt proposed to make a Mickey Mouse cartoon with sound. The result was *Steamboat Willie*, the world's first cartoon with sound. Mickey Mouse's voice, provided by Walt himself, soon became one of the most recognizable voices in the United States, and "Mickey Mouse Clubs"—at which children sang Mickey Mouse songs, traded souvenirs, and watched the latest cartoons—sprang up around the country. Soon, Mickey Mouse could be seen on everything from hairbrushes to pajamas, alarm clocks to doll houses.

Even with the widespread popularity of Mickey Mouse, Walt wasn't content to just sit back and enjoy the company's success. Another film industry innovation had caught his eye: color. In 1932, Walt Disney Productions created its first color cartoon, called *Flowers and Trees*, which won an Academy Award.

"You won't find anyone who can really explain the magic of Walt.... He was a common man who was endowed with a touch of magic."

Peter Ellenshaw,
Walt Disney Productions Artist

Mickey Mouse memorabilia (especially from the 1930s) is prized by collectors and can be very valuable

A Drive for Perfection

Walter Elias Disney was born on December 5, 1901, in Chicago, Illinois, the fourth of Elias and Flora Disney's five children. When Walt was five years old, his family moved to a farm in Marceline, Missouri, where Walt spent his days playing outdoors. Then, in 1911, the family moved again, this time to Kansas City, where Walt and his brother Roy got up at 3:30 every morning to deliver newspapers before school. Although other newspaper boys were allowed to throw the newspapers on people's lawns, Walt's father required his sons to put the papers behind the customers' storm doors. While the brothers hated the job at the time (nine-year-old Walt would often cry as he delivered the papers in the cold), it taught them a valuable lesson about making every customer happy and instilled in them a drive for perfection that later manifested itself in their business.

But Walt still wasn't satisfied. So far, all of the studio's cartoons had been shorts, designed to be shown before a live-action feature film. Now, Walt wanted to create an animated feature film, 20 times the length of a short. In 1934, the studio began work on *Snow White and the Seven Dwarfs*, despite the fact that people in the film industry said that no one would sit still for an hour and a half of cartoons and took to calling the movie "Disney's Folly."

After three years—and $1.5 million—*Snow White* opened at a theater in Los Angeles. Major movie stars of the day, including Charlie Chaplin, Shirley Temple, and George Burns, were on hand for the premiere of the world's first full-length animated movie. Although critics had warned that people would never believe that a cartoon boy and girl could fall in love, audience members were in tears when they thought *Snow White* had died. After its grand premiere, *Snow White* went on to earn $8 million, as well as an Academy Award—or rather, eight Academy Awards: one big one along with seven little ones for each of the dwarfs. Walt and Roy Disney had arrived.

2

An Expanding Empire

After the phenomenal success of *Snow White*, the Disneys set about reinvesting the money that the film had earned back into their company. Some of the money was used to build a new studio in Burbank, California, complete with volleyball and badminton courts, a restaurant and snack shop that delivered to employees' offices, and a gym on the roof.

In addition, a portion of the money was used to provide the company's animators with art lessons so that they could make even more spectacular feature-length films.

Soon after spending the money from *Snow White*, however, the company again found itself facing tough financial times. In 1939, Germany invaded Poland, sparking World War II. Suddenly, the foreign market—which accounted for nearly half of the company's business—disappeared. Then, in 1940, two new animated films, *Pinocchio* and *Fantasia*, brought in less money than they had cost to make.

Unwilling to lay off any of the company's 1,000 employees, Roy and Walt decided to sell stock in their company and in this way managed to raise enough money to stay in business. Despite the brothers' efforts, rumors of job cuts began to circulate, and many of the company's employees joined a labor union. In May 1941, nearly half of Disney's artists went on strike, marching outside the studio with signs calling Walt a slave driver.

Other employees refused to cross the picket line, although those who did enter the studio continued work on the company's next animated feature, *Dumbo*, which became a huge success. Finally, after more than a month, the strike was brought to an end with the agreement that, in the future, salaries would be negotiated by the Screen Cartoonists Guild. After that, the company's snack shop was closed, and employees were required to punch a time clock.

Shortly after the strike ended, Walt Disney Productions was faced with another crisis. On December 7, 1941, the Japanese bombed Pearl Harbor, Hawaii, in a surprise attack. Later that day, 700 soldiers took up residence in the studio in order to protect a nearby aircraft plant from attack. Besides providing a home for the soldiers, Walt Disney Productions also soon began to provide films for the government. With films to train soldiers, as well as shorts to educate the public about topics such as the importance of paying taxes, Walt Disney Productions eventually

Disney's *Snow White and the Seven Dwarfs* proved that animated films could be box-office successes created 38 miles' worth (61 km) of film for the war effort. Because these films were provided at cost, the company emerged from the war in 1945 almost $5 million in debt.

In an effort to keep the company going, the studio decided to broaden its film offerings. "I wanted it set up so that all my eggs were not in that cartoon basket," Walt said. In 1947, the company produced *Seal Island*, a 27-minute film that featured the antics of real Alaskan seals, set to funny narration and lively music. After the film won an Academy Award, the company decided that it would create more of these "True-Life Adventures." At the same time, the studio also began to make live-action films, such as *Treasure Island*, which was completed in 1950. In 1953, Walt Disney Productions set up its own company, called Buena Vista, to distribute its films.

Even as the Disneys' film business began to expand, Walt harbored another dream: to create a clean, safe amusement park for families. When Roy, who worried that the company knew nothing

"We keep moving forward, opening up new doors, and doing new things, because we're curious … and curiosity keeps leading us down new paths."

Walt Disney

Walt Disney Productions made public-service films and designed military badges during World War II about theme parks, told Walt that he couldn't use the company's money to finance his park, Walt emptied his own savings account, took out a loan against his life insurance policy, sold his second home in Palm Springs, and borrowed money from a number of employees. With this money, Walt founded Walt Disney, Incorporated (which later became WED Enterprises) in 1952. The new company's task was to design and build a theme park called Disneyland. As WED's employees, called "Imagineers," set to work on Disneyland, Walt turned to a new medium, television, to help make his dream park a reality.

In 1953, Walt made a deal with the ABC network: in return for $500,000 cash and $4.5 million in loans, Walt would give the

The 77-foot-tall (23.5 m) Sleeping Beauty Castle was designed as a centerpiece of Disneyland

Bringing Cartoons to Life

In Walt Disney's day, cartoons were still a relatively new creation. When Walt started working at the Kansas City Film Ad Company, which made cartoon ads for local businesses, in 1920, the company was making cartoons by pinning little paper figures to a board, filming them for a split second, then moving the figures and filming them again. Walt and other animators soon discovered, however, that drawn figures looked more realistic than paper ones. In order to make cartoons appear to move, animators draw a single frame of a movie. Then they draw another frame, with the characters in a slightly different position than they were in in the previous frame. After creating and filming thousands of such frames, the cartoon is run through a projector, and the drawings appear to move. Although much of today's animation is aided by computers, artistry and attention to detail are still important parts of making drawings come to life.

network a one-hour weekly series, as well as one-third ownership of Disneyland. In addition to securing much-needed financing for his park, Walt recognized that the arrangement also allowed him to reach more than four million Americans to promote his company. In October 1954, the television show *Disneyland* (named after the park) aired for the first time. Walt himself hosted the show, which featured animated cartoons, live-action miniseries about characters such as Davy Crockett and Zorro, and promotions for the new park.

As enthusiasm for the Disneyland theme park grew, Roy decided to invest the company's money in the project after all, and plans quickly moved forward. Featuring Sleeping Beauty Castle, Fantasyland, Adventureland, Frontierland, Tomorrowland, and an idyllic Main Street—modeled after Marceline, Missouri, the boyhood town of Walt and Roy Disney—Disneyland was designed as a dramatic departure from traditional theme parks. In August 1954, excavations for

Disneyland were begun in Anaheim, California, but with its opening day less than 11 months away, many wondered if the park could be completed in time.

3

End of an Era

Disneyland's opening on July 17, 1955, was less than perfect. The park was overcrowded—with an estimated 33,000 people in attendance—because someone had distributed fake invitations to the "invitation only" event. As a result, Disneyland's restaurants ran short on food, and water fountains ran dry."

To make matters worse, the park wasn't quite finished—some of the cement hadn't hardened, and there were piles of lumber stacked off to the sides of the attractions. In addition, one ride after another broke down. But the show had to go on, as it was being broadcast live across the country. Walt Disney later referred to the opening day of Disneyland as "Black Sunday," and for days after the disastrous opening, newspapers criticized the park. One reporter wrote, "It felt like a giant cash register clicking and clanging as creatures of Disney magic came tumbling down from their lofty places in my daydreams to peddle and perish their charms with the aggressiveness of so many curbside barkers."

Despite its rocky opening, Disneyland soon became a success, and by the end of 1955, more than a million people had visited the park. As was his custom, Walt refused to be satisfied with this success, insisting that the only way the park would continue to bring in people would be through "plussing"—his term for making ongoing improvements. "Disneyland will never be completed," he said. Only four years after its opening, the park was updated, with new rides such as the Submarine Voyage, the Matterhorn Mountain bobsled ride, and the Disney Monorail being added. Walt's plan to draw people back to the park again and again by adding new attractions proved successful: by 1965, 30 million people had visited Disneyland.

Along with the success of Disneyland came new successes in television and theater. In 1955, *The Mickey Mouse Club* debuted on television. Featuring "Mousketeers"—teenagers who wore Mickey Mouse ears and sang and danced—as well as cartoons and other segments. The show became a hit, with 75 percent of American households tuning in to it daily. Walt also continued to host his weekly *Disneyland* show, which ran under various names for 29 years, making it the longest-lasting prime-time television series of all time.

In movies, the studio switched its focus from animation to live action during the 1950s, largely

Disneyland opened in 1955 with five distinct park areas, including the jungle-themed Adventureland because live-action films cost less to make and generally brought in more money. Movies such as *The Great Locomotive Chase*, *The Shaggy Dog*, and *Westward Ho the Wagons!* did well at the box office, although none could match the stunning success of *Mary Poppins*, which premiered in 1964 and brought in $44 million and 13 Academy Award nominations.

Despite its new focus on live-action films, the studio also continued to produce animated features, although by the 1960s these were coming at a rate of one every four years. In 1959, *Sleeping Beauty* was completed at a cost of $6 million—the most the company had ever spent on an animated film. Although the movie is today considered among the best animated features ever made because of its artistry, it lost money in its original release.

By the 1960s, Walt was beginning to get bored with making movies, so he jumped at the chance to create four major attractions for the 1964 World's Fair in New York. For these

"You could go on the moon trip at Disneyland. You could visit the future! Disneyland was wondrous, because nobody had ever seen anything like it. It gave you the experience."

Gregory Benford,
Science Fiction Writer

Mary Poppins, starring Dick Van Dyke and Julie Andrews, is considered one of the best musical films ever

The 1971 opening of the $400-million (but still incomplete) Walt Disney World brought in 10,000 visitors the first day

Epco

The City of Celebration

Although the Walt Disney Company was never able to fully realize Walt Disney's dream of creating a city of the future, it took a step in that direction with Epcot. Then, in 1996, it took another step with the city of Celebration. Created on the undeveloped land of the Walt Disney World complex in Florida, Celebration is a real town designed to foster a sense of community among the approximately 8,000 ordinary citizens who live there. Unlike most suburbs, the houses in Celebration do not all look the same—in fact, no house is allowed to look identical to a neighboring house. And all of the houses in the city have to have an open front porch in order to encourage neighbors to interact. In addition, almost every house is within walking distance of the town center. Celebration is also focused on education, with an innovative public school, and on healthcare and wellness.

attractions—the Carousel of Progress, It's a Small World (a ride featuring singing dolls from around the world), the Magic Skyway, and Great Moments with Mr. Lincoln—Walt experimented with a new technology called Audio-Animatronics, which involved creating robot-like people and animals that moved by means of cogs, pulleys, and gears. The Audio-Animatronic Lincoln—who, along with It's a Small World and the Carousel of Progress, was brought back to Disneyland after the fair—could perform 48 different body actions and 15 facial movements.

After the World's Fair, Walt turned his attention to central Florida, where he had bought 43 square miles (111 sq km) of land on which he planned to build two new parks: Disney World, similar to California's Disneyland, and Epcot, which he imagined as the city of tomorrow. Then, in December 1966, just as plans for these parks were getting off the ground, Walt died of lung cancer. People around the world mourned for the man who had brought them Mickey Mouse.

CBS Evening News commentator Eric Sevareid spoke of Walt's legacy: "He was an original. Not just an American original, but an original, period.... People are saying we'll never see his like again."

Soon after Walt's death, people began to wonder if work on Disney World would be cancelled. Their questions were answered when construction on the park began in 1967 under the leadership of Roy Disney, who had taken over as chief executive officer (CEO) of Walt Disney Productions after Walt died. In October 1971, the park opened, with the new name of Walt Disney World; Roy insisted that his brother's first name be attached to the park "so people will always know that it was Walt's dream."

Only two months after the opening of Walt Disney World, in December 1971, Roy Disney died. For the first time in its history, Walt Disney Productions faced the prospect of operating without a Disney at the helm.

4

Troubled Times

After Roy's death, Card Walker, a longtime Disney employee who had started out as a messenger for the company in 1938, took over as president (he was later named CEO in 1976). Walker focused on keeping the family-oriented traditions of Walt Disney Productions and continually asked "What would Walt have done?"

Although Walker felt that asking this question before undertaking any new project enabled him to stay true to the Disneys' vision for their company, it also seemed to hamper creativity. As Roy Disney's son, Roy E. Disney, who was a producer at Walt Disney Productions, tried to convince Walker, "The thing about Walt was that he did it different each time. It's the creativity you have to imitate. And no drugstore in the world sells that."

Yet, the studio just couldn't seem to find the creativity that had once made it a legend in the film business. Instead, Walt Disney Productions turned out one forgettable movie after another, including four sequels to *The Love Bug*, a 1969 movie about a Volkswagen Beetle with a mind of its own. In animated movies, the company fared little better, as 1977's *Pete's Dragon* did poorly at the box office.

As a result of the creative drain in the company, in 1977, Roy E. Disney submitted his resignation, saying, "The creative atmosphere for which the Company has so long been famous and on which it prides itself has, in my opinion, become stagnant. I do not believe it is a place where I, and perhaps others, can realize our creative capacities." Two years later, more than 15 of the company's animators quit, complaining that the studio was no longer concerned about the quality that had once been the hallmark of Disney's animated features.

While the film studio was doing poorly, the theme parks were faring little better. With little money to spare, the company was unable to fulfill Walt's goal of constantly updating the rides at Walt Disney World and Disneyland, and attendance at the parks began to fall. At the same time, however, the company began work on Epcot near Walt Disney World. Rather than the futuristic city Walt had envisioned—where residents would live and work and test new, innovative products—the new plan for Epcot resembled a world's fair. The World Showcase featured pavilions celebrating the cultures and cuisines of countries

Although *The Love Bug* was the top-grossing movie of 1969, its numerous sequels were less successful around the world, while Future World showcased the products and gadgets of the future. The cost of building Epcot, which opened in October 1982, eventually soared to $1.2 billion, much more than original estimates.

While construction was taking place on Epcot in Florida, Walt Disney Productions also began its first attempt at a theme park overseas. At the request of a Japanese company, Walt Disney Productions designed Tokyo Disneyland to look and feel almost exactly like the original park in California. When the new park opened in April 1983, it met with wild success, although Disney saw only a percentage of the park's profits because it had declined to operate the park itself, instead

A futuristic-looking monorail was built to carry visitors throughout the vast, 260-acre (105 ha) Epcot serving only as an adviser to the Japanese company that owned the park.

Just before the opening of Tokyo Disneyland, Card Walker retired, turning the chief executive position over to Walt Disney's son-in-law Ron Miller, who had started out as an assistant director at the company in the 1950s. Faced with falling profits, Miller worked quickly to try to revive the film studio. After a study showed that teens weren't interested in Disney movies (a Chicago teen said he "wouldn't be caught dead" walking into one), Miller determined that the company needed another film label, separate from the Disney name, to produce and distribute movies for teens and adults. In 1984, Touchstone Pictures was established and released its first movie, *Splash*, which grossed $69 million, more than any other Disney film had made up to that time.

Despite the success of *Splash*, unrest continued at Disney. Because the company's stock prices were falling, Walt Disney Productions suddenly found itself vulnerable to a takeover

"At a certain level, what we do at Disney is very simple.... Above all, we tell stories, in the hope that they will entertain, inform, and engage."

Michael Eisner,
Former Disney CEO

Splash, the first Disney film created for older audiences, helped to make a movie star of actor Tom Hanks

Mickey's Changing Form

When Mickey Mouse was "born" in the late 1920s, he was a simple figure, with circles for his head, body, and ears. His feet were square, black boxes. From the beginning, though, Mickey was constantly changing. First, the animators decided to give him light-colored shoes, then they added the white gloves that became his hallmark. By the end of the 1930s, Mickey had a pear-shaped body, and pupils had been added to his eyes in order to make them more expressive. Unlike his appearance, Mickey's personality—based largely on Walt Disney himself—remained fairly constant. According to legendary Mickey Mouse animator Fred Moore, "Mickey seems to be the average young boy of no particular age; living in a small town, clean living, fun loving, bashful around girls, polite and as clever as he must be for the particular story."

by an outside investor, who could buy up the company's stock to take control of the whole corporation. In March 1984, an investor named Saul Steinberg began to purchase large amounts of Disney stock, with the intent of taking over the company—and then possibly selling off its assets to increase his profits. In order to prevent the company from being taken over, Walt Disney Productions bought back its stock, paying Steinberg $325.5 million—$31.7 million more than he had originally paid for it.

Afterward, Disney's stock prices dropped even lower, leading other investors to look for an opportunity to attempt a takeover as well. The company soon determined that in order to reduce the threat, it needed a management change. As a result, in September 1984, the company's board of directors—among them Roy E. Disney—asked Ron Miller to resign. In his place, they hired Michael Eisner, who had been working as president of Paramount Pictures, one of the biggest entertainment companies in the world.

They hoped that the creativity Eisner had poured into successful Paramount films such as *Star Trek*, *Grease*, and *Raiders of the Lost Ark* could help to revitalize their own operations.

5
Growth and Change

Michael Eisner stepped into his job as Disney's new leader with a sense of energy and urgency. Soon, the film studio was once again turning out successful live-action films, such as *Down and Out in Beverly Hills, Pretty Woman, and Honey, I Shrunk the Kids.* Eisner also put Roy E. Disney in charge of the animation department, which began to churn out hits as well in the late 1980s and early '90s, with *The Little Mermaid, Beauty and the Beast, Aladdin,* and *The Lion King.* It looked like Disney was finally back at the box office.

Not only was Disney again a hit in theaters, but the company also began to reappear in people's homes as Eisner struck a deal with ABC, which agreed to air a Disney movie every Sunday night. For those who wanted the opportunity to watch a Disney movie any time, the company began to sell its animated classics on video. In the early 1990s, the Walt Disney Company also began to stage live theatrical productions of its most recent animated films, such as *Beauty and the Beast*, which met with rave reviews from sold-out audiences.

Even while focusing on movies, television, and the stage, the Walt Disney Company didn't ignore its theme parks. In May 1989, the company opened the Disney-MGM Studios theme park (later renamed Disney's Hollywood Studios) near Walt Disney World in Florida. The new park included a working animation studio, attractions highlighting the history of motion pictures, and a stunt show. New rides were also added to Disneyland, and new, themed hotels were added to the Walt Disney World Resort complex.

Overseas, Disney also continued to expand, this time in Paris, France. In April 1992, more than 20,000 people attended the opening of Euro Disney (later renamed Disneyland Paris). Despite its strong opening, Disneyland Paris soon ran into trouble, and, as a result of falling attendance, the company was forced to lower the park's admission prices.

In spite of the financial troubles resulting from Disneyland Paris, in 1995, the Walt Disney Company purchased Capital Cities/ABC Television for $19 billion. In addition to ABC and its television programs, the acquisition included ABC News, ABC Sports, and ESPN, the leading cable sports network. Although the acquisition of ABC was widely praised, the Walt Disney Company soon found itself in trouble as the network was faced with falling ratings.

ABC's declining ratings weren't the Walt Disney Company's only problem, though. After the September 11, 2001, terrorist attacks on the World Trade Center and the Pentagon, tourism

Michael Eisner oversaw the so-called "Disney Renaissance" of great animated films in the 1990s collapsed and attendance at the company's theme parks decreased sharply. Shortly afterward, the company purchased the Fox Family cable TV channel (which it renamed ABC Family) for $5.2 billion, a price some criticized as too high, especially since the company had little to air on the channel aside from cheerleading competitions, a series about unsolved mysteries, and reruns of ABC's *According to Jim*.

At the same time, there was growing discontent with Eisner's management within the company, as the CEO began to micromanage, question others' decisions, and even task employees with spying on one another. In 2003, Roy E. Disney, who had once championed Eisner as the best candidate for the chief

The rides, shows, and attractions in Disney's Hollywood Studios theme Park all focus on movies and animation executive position, called for his resignation and began a campaign to try to convince shareholders to withhold their votes of confidence in Eisner at the company's 2004 annual meeting. The campaign was successful, and in March 2004, nearly 45 percent of the company's shareholders withheld their votes from Eisner. As a result, Eisner retired in October 2005, only weeks after presiding over the opening of the company's newest theme park: Hong Kong Disneyland.

Following Eisner's retirement, Robert Iger, who had served as president and chief operating officer under Eisner, was named chief executive. Within months of taking his new position, Iger announced the acquisition of Pixar Animation, a computer animation studio that had collaborated with Disney on such highly successful films as *Toy Story* and *Monsters, Inc.*

Iger also embraced new technology by making Disney the first to offer its movies and TV shows for download to iPods. "We are witnessing an explosion of media, and Disney is both reaping

"Even at 10 [years old] I could spot the difference between a Disney cartoon and all the others. I didn't know about the technical stuff, but I knew what my eyes told me."

Don Williams,
Walt Disney Company Illustrator

Toy Story, widely hailed as a masterpiece, helped usher in a new era of three-dimensional computer animation

Movies, Music, and Merchandise

Although it started out as a film studio, today, the Walt Disney Company is involved in nearly every aspect of the entertainment world. Because it has grown so large, the company is now divided into four business segments. The Disney Studio Entertainment division focuses on movies, as well as on the company's record labels, which include Hollywood Records and Lyric Street Records. Disney Parks and Resorts controls the company's theme parks as well as its two cruise ships, the Disney Magic and the Disney Wonder, which cater to families. Disney Consumer Products oversees the company's Disney Stores, which sell Disney merchandise. This division also runs Disney's publishing house, which is the world's largest publisher of children's books and magazines. Finally, Disney Media Networks encompasses the company's television networks, including ABC, ESPN, Disney Channel, ABC Family, and SOAPnet, as well as its radio networks, such as Radio Disney and ESPN Radio.

the benefits of that explosion and acting as a catalyst by taking a technology-friendly approach," Iger said.

In addition to continuing to expand into new technologies in the future, the Walt Disney Company is also looking to increase its presence overseas, especially in China, where it hopes to open a new theme park in Shanghai in 2012. In other countries, Disney plans to add an interactive Lilo & Stitch attraction to Disneyland Paris and a Monsters, Inc. ride to Tokyo Disneyland. In the U.S., the Toy Story Mania ride was slated to appear at both Disney's Hollywood Studios and Disney's California Adventure Park (part of the Disneyland Resort) by 2008.

With its expanded theme park offerings, as well as plans in the works for new computer-animated movies such as *Rapunzel* and *Toy Story 3*, the Walt Disney Company looks to continue its namesake's spirit of growth and adventure. And through it all, the company strives to remain faithful to the character whose ears have become one of the most recognized symbols in the world, fulfilling Walt's hope that his company would never "lose sight of one thing—it was all started by a mouse!"

Glossary

acquisition the purchase of one company by another company

animated films drawings produced on film and then shown through a projector so that they seem to move; animated films are also called cartoons

assets the various properties that a person or organization owns

barkers people who stand at the entrance to a show or fair and yell to passersby as a way to advertise the event

cogs teeth on the rim of a gear that connect with another gear to transmit movement from one gear to the other

cost the price it costs to make something; if a product is provided at cost, the company charges only what it cost to make the product and therefore doesn't make a profit

distributor a company that arranges for movie theaters to show movies made by another company

frame an individual still picture on a strip of film

grossed earned as profit, before subtracting the expenses involved in making the film

iPods portable media players manufactured by Apple Computer; iPods can play digital music and movie files

labor union an organization of employees who together negotiate salaries and other benefits with their employer

market a geographic region or segment of the population to which companies try to sell goods; for example, the North American market, the youth market, or the world market

medium a means of communicating information to the public, such as television, newspapers, radios, books, magazines, and movies; the plural is media

ratings an estimate of the number of people who watch a certain television show or network; higher ratings mean more viewers

shareholders people or corporations who own shares of stock (portions of ownership) in a corporation

short a movie lasting 30 minutes or less; from the early 1900s to the

1950s, shorts were often shown before a full-length movie

stagnant not moving forward or making progress

stock shared ownership in a company by many people who buy shares, or portions, of stock, hoping the company will make a profit and the stock value will increase

tuberculosis an infectious disease that mainly affects the lungs and causes high fever, cough, and difficulty breathing

votes of confidence votes that express confidence in a leader and approval of his or her performance; withholding a vote of confidence signifies disapproval and the wish for new leadership

World's Fair an international fair featuring exhibits and participants from around the world

Selected Bibliography

Eisner, Michael D., and Tony Schwartz. Work in Progress. New York: Random House, 1998.

Ford, Barbara. Walt Disney. New York: Walker and Company, 1989.

Greene, Katherine and Richard. The Man Behind the Magic: The Story of Walt Disney. New York: Viking, 1991.

Grover, Ron. The Disney Touch: Disney, ABC & the Quest for the World's Greatest Media Empire. Chicago: Irwin Professional Publishing, 1997.

———. The Disney Touch: How a Daring Management Team Revived an Entertainment Empire. Homewood, Ill.: Business One Irwin, 1991.

Richardson, Adele. The Story of Disney. Mankato, Minn.: Smart Apple Media, 2004.

Stewart, James B. Disney War. New York: Simon & Schuster, 2005.

Index

JAICO PUBLISHING HOUSE

Elevate Your Life. Transform Your World.

ESTABLISHED IN 1946, Jaico Publishing House is home to world-transforming authors such as Sri Sri Paramahansa Yogananda, Osho, The Dalai Lama, Sri Sri Ravi Shankar, Sadhguru, Robin Sharma, Deepak Chopra, Jack Canfield, Eknath Easwaran, Devdutt Pattanaik, Khushwant Singh, John Maxwell, Brian Tracy and Stephen Hawking.

Our late founder Mr. Jaman Shah first established Jaico as a book distribution company. Sensing that independence was around the corner, he aptly named his company Jaico ('Jai' means victory in Hindi). In order to service the significant demand for affordable books in a developing nation, Mr. Shah initiated Jaico's own publications. Jaico was India's first publisher of paperback books in the English language.

While self-help, religion and philosophy, mind/body/spirit, and business titles form the cornerstone of our non-fiction list, we publish an exciting range of travel, current affairs, biography, and popular science books as well. Our renewed focus on popular fiction is evident in our new titles by a host of fresh young talent from India and abroad. Jaico's recently established Translations Division translates selected English content into nine regional languages.

In addition to being a publisher and distributor of its own titles, Jaico is a major national distributor of books of leading international and Indian publishers. With its headquarters in Mumbai, Jaico has branches and sales offices in Ahmedabad, Bangalore, Bhopal, Chennai, Delhi, Hyderabad, Kolkata and Lucknow.

SINCE 1946